S0-AED-021

Christmas cookies

Edible Treats for Your Body & Soul

Joe S. Jones

¡Merry Christmas!

WORD & SPIRIT
PUBLISHING

www.wordandspiritpublishing.com

Unless otherwise indicated, all Scripture quotations are taken from the *Holy Bible, New International Version®*. Copyright © 1973, 1978, 1984 by International Bible Society. Used by permission of Zondervan Publishing House. All rights reserved worldwide.

Scripture quotations marked "AMP" are taken from the Amplified® Bible, copyright © 1954, 1958, 1962,1964,1965,1987 by The Lockman Foundation. Used by permission.

Scripture quotations from The Message. Copyright © by Eugene H. Peterson, 1993, 1994, 1995, 1996, 200, 2001, 2002. Used by permission of NavPress Publishing Group.

Christmas Cookies: Edible Treats for Your Body & Soul

ISBN: 978-1-9395703-0-7

Copyright © 2013
Joe S. Jones and The Landing

Check out Joe's daily blog, Cup of Joe at www.cupofjoe.tv

Published by Word & Spirit Publishing.
PO Box 701403
Tulsa, OK 74170
www.wordandspiritpublishing.com

All rights reserved under International Copyright Law. Contents and/or cover may not be reproduced in whole or in part in any form without the express written consent of the Publisher. Printed in the United States of America.

Introduction

I t's the most wonderful time of the year! The songs, the lights, the occasional snow, the shopping. Well, I don't really like the shopping that much! One of the things that makes Christmas more special than any other time of the year is the festive gatherings and the joy-filled celebrations. Companies have parties, people exchange gifts, and for the most part, everyone seems to be in a much better mood. That is, unless they are at the mall and stuck in the midst of the chaos at the checkout lines! When it comes to fully devoted followers of Jesus, I think that we should have the biggest parties of all. After all, it is the birth of our Lord and Savior that is the centerpiece of the Christmas season!

Another delightful part of the holiday season are the Christmas cookies. I am certain that you have your favorites. These edible treats only appear at Christmastime, which makes us want them even more as the holiday approaches. In fact, I look forward to December because I know the entire month will be filled with sweet smells and tasty treats. Every year during this season I also like to go back and nibble on a few edible treats from the Word of God—spiritual "cookies" as I call them—my favorite scriptures that feed my soul and lift my spirits.

In 2008 I began a series called *Christmas Cookies:Edible Treats for Your Body and Soul.* This has become an annual event for me and for those at The Landing Community Church. To commemorate five years of sweet goodness, we have put together a dozen of our favorite treats from the Bible and a dozen of the tastiest recipes from our friends and families that are sure to encourage you and satisfy your sweet tooth. Enjoy!

Cookie #1

2 Peter 1:3-11

His divine power has given us everything we need for a godly life through our knowledge of him who called us by his own glory and goodness. Through these he has given us his very great and precious promises, so that through them you may participate in the divine nature, having escaped the corruption in the world caused by evil desires.

For this very reason, make every effort to add to your faith goodness; and to goodness, knowledge; and to knowledge, self-control; and to self-control, perseverance; and to perseverance, godliness; and to godliness, mutual affection; and to mutual affection, love. For if you possess these qualities in increasing measure, they will keep you from being ineffective and unproductive in your knowledge of our Lord Jesus Christ. But whoever does not have them is nearsighted and blind, forgetting that they have been cleansed from their past sins.

Therefore, my brothers and sisters, make every effort to confirm your calling and election. For if you do these things, you will never stumble, and you will receive a rich welcome into the eternal kingdom of our Lord and Savior Jesus Christ.

This little cookie has so many wonderful ingredients. It reminds me of one of those square 7-layer treats that is so good, you have to nibble because you just can't handle a full bite. From *faith* to *love*, and all of the other layers in between, this cookie has it all. You see, God gave us promises. Those promises help us to be participants in His divine nature. By participating in His agenda we can escape corruption, and all of the evil and dark things of this world. Evil desires will not have a hold on us because we will not even be in the same place as they are. If we *possess* these qualities we are going to succeed! Recipes are used for a reason . . . because we can forget ingredients, and to forget something could be damaging to the end result. In the same way, you and I must make certain that all of these godly ingredients get into our life every day.

Faith is necessary—without it God is not pleased. But faith without works . . . is dead.

Goodness. Being a good person is a wonderful characteristic, but without **knowledge, self-control,** and **perseverance,** "good" will not be good enough.

Godliness. Living a godly life is incredible, but without **being kind** and **loving your brothers and sisters in Christ** (and those not yet in Christ), we are just going through the motions.

All of the above ingredients must be added in the proper measure to produce the "cookie" that you like to eat. And the thing about this spiritual Christmas cookie—it is part of the mixture that allows you to keep being effective and productive and pleasing to those in your circle of influence.

So follow me here: the promises of God are given to you so that through them you can participate in the plan that God has for you. That plan has a recipe . . . a deep dish of faith and seven layers: seven ingredients that must be measured out and thoroughly blended together. By doing so, we escape corruption and evil desires because we are walking in a different direction. When the mixture is ready, all that remains is subjecting it to the heat for some time and allowing the heat to complete the process. The heat does not hurt them . . . it shapes them. Heat brings out the best in our Christmas cookies. In life it's the heat, the trials and the tests, that should bring out the best in us too! We should continue to rise . . . to be effective . . . to be producers. As my mom's cookies would bake, the house would be

God's plan has a recipe . . . a deep dish of faith and seven layers: seven ingredients that must be measured out and thoroughly blended together.

filled with the aroma of what she was baking. The longer they baked, the more I craved what was coming. I would look forward to the bell that signaled the heating time was over and they were finally ready. She would take them out, line them up on wax paper or a cooling tray, and then we would wait with anticipation for a moment or two before we began enjoying the tasty treats.

The aroma, all of the ingredients, following the recipe . . . it all led to the best Christmas cookie ever. And why shouldn't it? Go back to that first verse. His divine power has given to us everything we need to live a godly life.

Cookie #2

James 1:2-8

Consider it pure joy, my brothers and sisters, whenever you face trials of many kinds, because you know that the testing of your faith produces perseverance. Let perseverance finish its work so that you may be mature and complete, not lacking anything. If any of you lacks wisdom, you should ask God, who gives generously to all without finding fault, and it will be given to you. But when you ask, you must believe and not doubt, because the one who doubts is like a wave of the sea, blown and tossed by the wind. That person should not expect to receive anything from the Lord. Such a person is double-minded and unstable in all they do.

The author of the book of James was the half-brother of Jesus. He was a devout man and a man of prayer; a man interested in developing the lifestyle of the believer. James is one of my favorite books . . . James 1 talks about the test of faith; James 2 about the nature of faith; James 3 about the works of faith; and chapters 4 and 5 deal with the application of faith. I wish I could talk about the whole book, but I'm dealing with cookies: bite size treats from the living, edible Word of God.

So let's jump right into this recipe and see what the Lord is cooking up for us.

"**Consider it pure joy**" . . . you may have a version that says *count it all joy*. **Consider it** . . . when you consider something you take time out to ponder and reflect on the magnitude of the idea or the thought. Whenever life takes a turn that we are not in favor of, we often begin to think about how bad our circumstances are. We consider the time we will lose, the money that we will or have lost, the detour that must be taken, and how far that will take us out of our way. James is speaking to all of the twelve tribes scattered abroad. This is a shotgun sermon to all the church. *Consider it pure joy* . . . even when things are not going the way you had intended.

Now before you start questioning how in the world you can be joyful when things are not going well, James gives us the reason. Consider it pure joy when you face trials of many kinds . . . why? Because the testing of your faith (*the challenge to your belief system*) develops **perseverance**. When I see that word perseverance I automatically think about what I must do to hang in there. But the NKJV uses a different word. It says **Patience.** I like that word better. I am supposed to learn that *patience works* . . . even when I am unable to. And I must let patience do her thing. Again, James tells us why . . . patience must finish her work so that we may be mature (perfect), complete, not lacking anything.

The fact of the matter is that you naturally get stronger when you face adversity. Without a test there can be no real testimony. Without a conflict there can be no conquest. Without a mess there can be no message. A trial is supposed to bring out the best in us and develop us into more of what God designed us to be. Trials lead to triumphs! For that to occur we have to be willing to consider the trials as "pure joy" moments.

I know this detour feels inconvenient. You don't know how far out of the way you are going or how much time you will lose. But consider the fact that God may be shielding you

Trust the Lord. Trust His heart and His timing. As you let patience develop, you become mature . . . or perfect in God's eyes . . . complete, lacking nothing. No Thing.

from something awful, perhaps even life threatening. If you knew that it could have been fatal going that direction and God brought you a detour, a delay to spare your life, chances are you would be able to consider that a joyful thing. You don't know what you don't know! Be patient. Trust the Lord. Trust His heart and His timing. As you let patience develop, you become mature . . . or perfect in God's eyes . . . complete, lacking nothing. **No thing.**

Now look at verse 5. Perhaps James knew that some of us would still not understand. "If any of you lack **wisdom**" . . . he should talk to God about it; ask for it; for God gives liberally, generously to all without showing any partiality. All you have to do is *ask*. Right there in the Word it confirms that when you ask you will receive. You see *faith must be shown if faith is to be known.* James not only wants us to get the secret formula for this recipe. He wants to make it very clear that there is a right way and a wrong way to talk to God about the things that you believe you don't have: things that you do not understand.

"When he asks, he must believe and not doubt." How many times does our heart believe and yet our mouth speaks against it? When you go to God about this stuff you have to go all in; you jump in with both feet. There is no room for doubt. Doubt is like a wave in the sea that tosses you around. You are no longer in control—the wave is. When you doubt you no longer drive the ship, doubt does. We need more people that are developed in their faith . . . folks that speak to the wind rather than be tossed by it. The wind does not control you: you control the wind.

It's time to see ourselves the way He created us: faith-filled; able to look at various trials and storms and count them as productive situations that will make us stronger, healthier, and more like Him. I cannot tell you how important it is to learn how to talk to God. We must learn the art of asking; moving to another level to seek and then to knock. If you are short on wisdom, ask God because there is an abundant supply

> It's time to see ourselves the way He created us: faith-filled . . .

that He wants to give you. Once you ask for it, believe that you have received it. How do you do that? Do something that moves you in the direction of the thing you were confused about. Start a conversation. Take a step. Move forward. Let that wisdom begin to find application to your situation.

Sometimes we talk ourselves right out of a miracle; right out of a blessing. Doubt kills faith. Doubt kills *you*. Look at what verse 7 says about those that give in to doubtful thoughts: "That person should not expect to receive anything from the Lord. Such a person is double-minded and unstable in **all** they do." I don't think there is any way that I can expound on that— it says it all. I must put doubt under if faith is to rise.

So don't jump to conclusions when things go a different way. Don't allow yourself to get all bent out of shape. Let God shape you. Let God use the trial you are facing to make something stronger and more beautiful. If I were to take the ingredients of our cookies out individually, they would not always be appetizing. But when all of them are put together in the right proportion, *mmm, mmm, good*! Let God test your character and let patience do her thing. You will be glad you did!

Cookie #3

Deuteronomy 28:1-14

If you fully obey the Lord your God and carefully follow all his commands I give you today, the Lord your God will set you high above all the nations on earth. All these blessings will come on you and accompany you if you obey the Lord your God:

You will be blessed in the city and blessed in the country.

The fruit of your womb will be blessed, and the crops of your land and the young of your livestock—the calves of your herds and the lambs of your flocks.

Your basket and your kneading trough will be blessed.

You will be blessed when you come in and blessed when you go out.

The Lord will grant that the enemies who rise up against you will be defeated before you. They will come at you from one direction but flee from you in seven.

The Lord will send a blessing on your barns and on everything you put your hand to. The Lord your God will bless you in the land he is giving you.

The Lord will establish you as his holy people, as he promised you on oath, if you keep the commands of the Lord your God and walk in obedience to him. Then all the peoples on earth will see that you are *called by the name of the Lord, and they will fear you. The Lord will grant you abundant prosperity—in the fruit of your womb, the young of your livestock and the crops of your ground—in the land he swore to your ancestors to give you.*

The Lord will open the heavens, the storehouse of his bounty, to send rain on your land in season and to bless all the work of your hands. You will lend to many nations but will borrow from none. The Lord will make you the head, not the tail. If you pay attention to the commands of the Lord your God that I give you this day and carefully follow them, you will always be at the top, never at the bottom. Do not turn aside from any of the commands I give you today, to the right or to the left, following other gods and serving them.

This spiritual cookie is enticing to me because of all the ingredients. It's full of promise. But the promise is not open ended—it comes with some conditions. The very first word, verse 1: *If.* If what? If you obey the Lord? No, if you *fully* obey the Lord. There is a huge difference in obedience and being fully obedient. Being in church or *fully* in church. It denotes a deeper commitment. Call it being sold out the whole route. Look at a plate of ham and eggs—the chicken was involved, but the pig was *fully* committed!

But wait! There's another condition: and carefully *follow* his commands—no, *all* of his commands. There is a difference in following directions and following *all* the directions. When these cookies are made, the directions have to be followed. You cannot take a shortcut. Some folks, like me, try to cook without truly measuring the ingredients. They eyeball it; use a pinch instead of a teaspoon. If you live your life like that, things may work well some of the time, but I can assure you that it will not work well *all* of the time. There are things we must do . . . we must be in position to take advantage of what the Lord is cooking for us. And when you are *fully* obeying and following *all* of the commands . . . well, here's where the flavor really comes out!

Look at a plate of ham and eggs—the chicken was involved, but the pig was **fully** committed!

All of these **blessings** shall come upon you. The good stuff starts to take over your life! Imagine being overwhelmed by blessing rather than trouble! He says *you* will be blessed in the city and blessed in the country. Urban, rural, it does not matter, for blessings are not limited to your locale. They follow *you* and overtake *you*, not your location.

The fruit of your womb will be blessed. Your kids . . . you birth 'em, He'll bless 'em! The crops of your land are blessed. Anything that you plant into the ground is blessed. Your tithes and your offerings; your gifts to friends and family. Wherever you plant you are blessed. The young of your livestock. Your children's children are blessed. The grandkids are now *"In His hand"* kids.

The calves of your herds and the lambs of your flocks will be blessed. The folks that your family and your children have influence upon, those in your circle, those that you connect with are blessed! Imagine folks being blessed just because they are in relationship with you! That's what this verse says—taste it and see that the Lord is good!

Your basket and kneading trough; your breads and fruits—you will have a blessed provision of all that you need to survive. You will always have something to eat! Blessed when you come in and blessed when you go out. Dine in, dine out . . . it just doesn't matter because God is going to overwhelm you with favor and blessings!

Now when you are living this kind of *blessed* life, you have got to know that the wrong people and spirits will come after you. You will have some battles, but look at verse 7: "The enemies who rise up against you will be defeated before you" (*not always by you*). I want you to get that. Some of the battles you will have to fight, but others you will *watch* being won right before your very eyes. In fact, when enemies come at you head-on and see the size of your God, and you *fully* obeying Him and following *all* of His commands, they will run away in every direction!

The Lord will establish you—that's stability.

The blessing of God will be upon the place you store all of your treasures—your home and your land. God blesses your property. Your bedroom, living room, kitchen, even your deck . . . blessed by God! Everything that you put your hand to . . . guess what it is? *Blessed*!

The Lord will **establish** you—that's stability. You don't waver between opinions. You are solid and founded upon what He says. Verse 11 says that He will grant you **abundant prosperity**! Now don't just tie that to your money . . . it applies to *all* of the things we have talked about. Your kids, your grandkids, your home, your job, your land. God *will* **open the heavens** . . . rain is coming. There is a shower of blessing coming upon your life. You will have what you need to take care of yourself and your family. You will even have some to help others. You will be the *head* and not the *tail*. You are going to come out not just on top, but over the top!

So the take away is that the world notices the blessing and favor of God's children. **Fully** devoted followers of Christ, born-again believers seeing and experiencing an ambush of blessing from God because when it comes to living for Him they are *all in*. If you really want to experience a delightful and tasty holiday, you need to find your favorite cookies. Spiritual cookies, Christmas cookies—the best part of this is that you can eat them anytime and they always satisfy! So follow the recipe, mix thoroughly, let the heat bring the shape and smell the goodness that God is cooking up for you!

Cookie #4

Romans 4:16-22

Therefore, the promise comes by faith, so that it may be by grace and may be guaranteed to all Abraham's offspring—not only to those who are of the law but also to those who have the faith of Abraham. He is the father of us all. As it is written: "I have made you a father of many nations." He is our father in the sight of God, in whom he believed—the God who gives life to the dead and calls into being things that were not.

Against all hope, Abraham in hope believed and so became the father of many nations, just as it had been said to him, "So shall your offspring be." Without weakening in his faith, he faced the fact that his body was as good as dead—since he was about a hundred years old—and that Sarah's womb was also dead. Yet he did not waver through unbelief regarding the promise of God, but was strengthened in his faith and gave glory to God, being fully persuaded that God had power to do what he had promised. This is why "it was credited to him as righteousness."

We see every year just what it means to stand on the promises of God. It's the way you find that highway of God's favor—the HOV lane, **H**urled **O**n to **V**ictory! Some of the greatest cookies are the most simple. Less can mean more. Less time at work, more time with the family. Less expense, more savings. Abraham believed God. There are many things in our lives that could dramatically change if we could simply *believe* God. Stepping out in faith is credited to our account as righteousness. It's a gold star . . . a big A+!

Blessed are those whose sins are forgiven and covered. (vs. 7)

Blessed are those whose sin the Lord will never count against them. (vs. 8)

Standing against the emotional sets us up
to stand in the midst of the spiritual.

Abraham **believed** the promise. Before you stand on it you have to believe it. You cannot learn from a source you don't trust. Let me break down some things you and I need to know about the promise. (vs. 16)

We are the seed of Abraham.

The promise he received is ours as well.

The promise comes by faith.

The promise is given by God and guaranteed.

You cannot earn this . . . it is a gift that will come to you from God as you move in faith. That means that you and I may have to take steps and make choices based on what our spirit tells us rather than what our eyes can see. But that's OK, because Jesus came to give us life . . . abundant life . . . a wonderful life. And Jesus was able to call things that were not as though they were. So when you and I get hold of this kind of faith, we can step out on nothing and find something there by the time our foot lands. Abraham was able to activate this in his life because he had reprogrammed his mind. He had a different way of thinking.

"Against all hope, in hope believed."

We cannot begin to believe in what God has for us until we let go of what we think we need for ourselves.

Standing against the emotional sets us up to stand in the midst of the spiritual.

There are some very basic, fundamental things that were part of this Abraham mindset that you and I can adopt as well. This recipe was passed down to us through the Bible and is available for consumption right now. If we will change our thinking, God can change our life! Here is Abraham's recipe for righteousness.

It's the Christmas story. . . .
He did not weaken in his faith.

He knew the promise and he moved towards it. So too did

the wise men who saw a star in the east and followed that star to find Jesus. They did not give up till they arrived at the stable.

He did not waver through unbelief.

Doubt cannot rise alongside of faith. As faith rises, doubt will diminish. Sometimes we just have to face the facts and then forget them! The wise men saw the star and pressed forward to worship the baby born King of the Jews.

He gave glory to God.

You can only fully glorify God when you become fully persuaded that He is able to do what He said He would do. Faith is strengthened, as we believe in the power of the promise. The wise men were full of joy when they saw the baby and they gave him gifts (worship) of gold, frankincense, and myrrh. Not only did they glorify God with their giving, God then warned them about the direction of their trip in a dream. Provision and protection are yours.

This is why Abraham was *credited with being righteous.* He followed the recipe and enjoyed the fruit of obedience. And because we are the seed of Abraham, we too can follow the recipe and enjoy all that was **promised.** Why not share this little Christmas story with someone you know this year?

Cookie #5

Isaiah 9:1-7 NLT

Nevertheless, that time of darkness and despair will not go on forever. The land of Zebulun and Naphtali will be humbled, but there will be a time in the future when Galilee of the Gentiles, which lies along the road that runs between the Jordan and the sea, will be filled with glory.

The people who walk in darkness will see a great light. For those who live in a land of deep darkness, a light will shine. You will enlarge the nation of Israel, and its people will rejoice.

They will rejoice before you as people rejoice at the harvest and like warriors dividing the plunder. For you will break the yoke of their slavery and lift the heavy burden from their shoulders. You will break the oppressor's rod, just as you did when you destroyed the army of Midian. The boots of the warrior and the uniforms bloodstained by war will all be burned. They will be fuel for the fire.

For a child is born to us, a son is given to us. The government will rest on his shoulders. And he will be called: Wonderful Counselor, Mighty God, Everlasting Father, Prince of Peace. His government and its peace will never end. He will rule with fairness and justice from the throne of his ancestor David for all eternity. The passionate commitment of the Lord of Heaven's Armies will make this happen!

The Christmas story is all about promise. The promise of a King. The hope of a people: Israel. If there is one thing that we realize the longer we live for the Lord, it is that He makes all the difference in the world. We know that where the Spirit of the Lord is, there is liberty! My God shall supply *all* of my need according to His riches in glory! I *can* do *all* things through Christ who strengthens me. The prophet Isaiah foretold of the miracle that would take place in Luke Chapter 2. It was a promise—this baby would be the hope of the people.

Jesus called things that were not as though they were. He created out of what He saw in the spirit. Let's talk for a minute about *naming your baby*. One of the most important things you do for your child is name them. Some folks name their first child after their father or a grandfather, and it would seem some folks do not put a lot of thought into the name. They may spend time choosing a name, but do not consider what that means to their child. Every name has a meaning. My name is Joseph, which means "increase" and "he shall add." So let me "add" a little more to help increase your faith!

My God shall supply all of my need according to His riches in glory! I can do all things through Christ who strengthens me.

The text we read tells us that darkness does not last forever. Bad things happen to good people, but the darkness is
going to leave and the light is coming! (Read verses 2-4 again.)
God was orchestrating a way to redeem His creation and to
make certain that mankind had every chance for success. So
this prophecy foretold of a baby. A Son is given, God's only
Son. And the government would be upon His shoulders; it
shall rest upon Him. Order, authority, power, protection, and
preservation—it all is found in Him. How do we know? Because this baby was named . . . named by God. Let's look at
what He was called.

Wonderful Counselor

There is no better place to take our trouble than to a person who gives great counsel. The first name given to Christ
reveals his innate ability to talk us through difficulty; to calm us
down; to redirect us if necessary. He is a wonderful counselor.
"Call upon me and I will answer. Seek me and **you will** find
me. Come to me all you who are weary and loaded down with
troubles and I will give you a lighter load."

Mighty God

This name speaks of His power. Power to change lives;
power to charge lives. When we are weak, He is strong. Our
weapons are not man-made, they are mighty through God. It's
divine power that we have *in His name*. He is almighty. He is
more powerful than any adversity. He is stronger than any force.

Everlasting Father

A father figure is somewhat self-explanatory. The father always cares for the needs of their child. Whatever the child asks for, the father does his best to help secure. Unfortunately in our culture, many people grow up without a father's influence. That is why this baby was born and given the name of everlasting father. He will always be there when others are not. He is a father to the fatherless. He is a father that lasts forever.

Prince of Peace

Peace is something special today. There is much chaos and confusion in this world. The world talks about peace, but it is not the same peace that comes in this name. His name *means* peace; His name *brings* peace. How lovely on the mountains are the feet of Him who brings good news, announcing peace and proclaiming news of happiness. He is the Prince of Peace!

His wisdom, power, authority, and peace will never end. That is how God named His baby. Now go back to that verse we referred to at the beginning: *Jesus calling things that were not yet as though they already were.* You and I are carrying a baby—purpose, dreams, goals, and aspirations. God placed them in you just as certainly as He placed Jesus on this earth and walked Him towards Calvary. You are pregnant with purpose. Sometime very soon this baby is coming forth. It's time for you to name it. What will you call your baby?

My dream, my baby, I named The Landing Community Church. Its vision would be to bring community to the church and the church to the community. It would be a safe place to land for those in a spiritual holding pattern. This baby would

He will always be there when others are not.

He is a father to the fatherless.

He is a father that lasts forever.

enrich and encourage, equip and empower, engage and evangelize those that had a relationship with it. And this baby would grow! Jesus grew too. He went about doing good and healing *all* that were oppressed by the devil. And today, He intercedes for you and me from heaven. He *is* the Wonderful Counselor, Mighty God, Everlasting Father, and Prince of Peace.

Cookie #6

Proverbs 3:1-10 NLT

My child, never forget the things I have taught you. Store my commands in your heart. If you do this, you will live many years, and your life will be satisfying.

Never let loyalty and kindness leave you! Tie them around your neck as a reminder. Write them deep within your heart. Then you will find favor with both God and people, and you will earn a good reputation.

Trust in the Lord with all your heart; do not depend on your own understanding. Seek his will in all you do, and he will show you which path to take.

Don't be impressed with your own wisdom. Instead, fear the Lord and turn away from evil. Then you will have healing for your body and strength for your bones.

Honor the Lord with your wealth and with the best part of everything you produce. Then he will fill your barns with grain, and your vats will overflow with good wine.

This cookie, this little tasty treat is all about a relationship of **trust**. This edible Word comes directly out of the pages of the Book of Proverbs: wise sayings from Solomon, who is considered by many to be the wisest person who ever lived. The proverbs were written to teach people wisdom and discipline. They were handed down to give insight so that we could live successful lives—to have that abundant life that Jesus came to give us. Chapter 1 it tells us that these words *will* give insight to the simple and knowledge and discernment to those that are young. (Proverbs 1:4)

To really enjoy a cookie, you need to **savor the flavor.** You don't eat it all in one bite; you take smaller bites and enjoy all of the ingredients that went in to make it what it is. The end result is an enjoyable, sweet treat. There are some instructions in the recipe for a long life—a long and satisfying life for you and me. Let's take a closer look at the ingredients.

Store my commands in your heart.

Your heart is like a pantry. The pantry holds all of the things that we use to put together our Christmas cookies. The things that the Lord has given to us through His Word, through prophecy and through personal revelation are to be stored in the pantry of our heart.

I think about this as a reminder to keep important things in your home. Your home should be a safe haven, a fortress, a refuge. But notice what it says in verse 3:

Never let loyalty and kindness leave you! Tie them around your neck as a reminder. Write them deep within your heart.

You take these good Words with you and like a scarf you bind them around your neck. Notice that the scarf protects your throat—the conduit by which you speak—so when you have a healthy supply of the Lord's commands in your pantry and on your person, your words will be guarded. You won't speak words of doubt or harmful things because loyalty and kindness are right there with you!

Then you will find favor with both God and people, and you will earn a good reputation.

Then you will find favor . . . and can I tell you, favor will find you too! *So you savor the flavor and enjoy the favor!* You'll earn a good reputation. Let's move on to the **Trust** I referred to earlier.

Trust in the Lord with all your heart; do not depend on your own understanding. Seek his will in all you do, and he will show you which path to take. Don't be impressed with your own wisdom. Instead, fear the Lord and turn away from evil. Then you will have healing for your body and strength for your bones.

You can deduce from this scripture that when you place your trust in the Lord, your body will be made whole. Again, you cannot fully trust someone you do not fully know. Trust is exercised by depending on Him, by looking for His way and His purpose. Not trying to figure everything out on your own. You see it's how well we rely on Him that determines how well we get along in our life.

Savor the flavor and enjoy the favor!

There is a reason to store up commands in the pantry of your heart. It's so that they can be used to guide you, guard you, and to give glory to God in each and every situation. The pantry does not always remain full. You have to keep putting things in there if you are going to keep making things. Which brings us to this last piece of wisdom:

Honor the Lord with your wealth and with the best part of every-thing you produce. Then he will fill your barns with grain, and your vats will overflow with good wine.

Our time, our talents and our treasure (our wealth) have been given to us by God. Our job was orchestrated by the Lord. Our paycheck is provided by God. What God requires of us is that we give back to Him: the first fruits; the first tasting of the great cookies that come out of our kitchens.

By giving back to Him we honor Him. And to honor Him we must first humble ourselves and realize that every good and perfect gift comes from Him. He will fill our barns with grain—grain is what you need to live. Your pantries will be full so that you can eat and so that you can help others eat too! Barns that are full and vats that are overflowing with *new* wine. God cannot give you another supply until you properly use the supply that you have already been given.

What are your favorite cookies?

If you really want to experience a delightfully tasty holiday, you need to find your own cookies—spiritual cookies and Christmas cookies. The best part is that you can taste His Word anytime and you will always be satisfied. So follow the recipes. Mix thoroughly and let the heat begin to shape you and bring out all that is good in you. Taste and see what the Lord has been cookin'!

C**o**okie #7

Ephesians 3:4-10 The Message

As you read over what I have written to you, you'll be able to see for yourselves into the mystery of Christ. None of our ancestors understood this. Only in our time has it been made clear by God's Spirit through his holy apostles and prophets of this new order. The mystery is that people who have never heard of God and those who have heard of him all their lives (what I've been calling outsiders and insiders) stand on the same ground before God. They get the same offer, same help, same promises in Christ Jesus. The Message is accessible and welcoming to everyone, across the board.

This is my life work: helping people understand and respond to this Message. It came as a sheer gift to me, a real surprise, God handling all the details. When it came to presenting the Message to people who had no background in God's way, I was the least qualified of any of the available Christians. God saw to it that I was equipped, but you can be sure that it had nothing to do with my natural abilities.

And so here I am, preaching and writing about things that are way over my head, the inexhaustible riches and generosity of Christ. My task is to bring out in the open and make plain what God, who created all this in the first place, has been doing in secret and behind the scenes all along. Through followers of Jesus like yourselves gathered in churches, this

extraordinary plan of God is becoming known and talked about even among the angels!

Here we are again: basking in the presence of the Lord during the holiday season with hearts that are full and noses that are filled with the aroma of fresh baked goodies. It's time for another Christmas cookie!

In 2011 at our church, we began the year by unveiling our keyword: **Illuminate**. We are the light of the world and especially during this season we need to let that light enhance, enlighten, and expose hope, revelation, and truth. So lets go to Paul's letter to the Ephesians and we will find some things that will benefit us by hearing and remembering. There are 5 things from our text that will help us remember God's incredible plan, His extraordinary people, and the role we all play in shining His light to the world.

We begin at verse 4 where Paul explains that we should be able to see for ourselves what God is up to by reading the words that Paul writes. I think that many times the answers to the questions we have are right in front of us but we fail to take the time to read, pray, and meditate upon the words. We have got to be able to see this for ourselves. We need our own experience. I want my own cookie!

Point 1 is that **we all stand on the same ground**. Those who have heard about Him and those who have not; insiders and outsiders; we are all on the same planet and occupying space. Some of us are in more developed areas, but we have a common denominator: we are all created in the image of God and born with a special reason for existing in the world. As Paul put it, we get the same offer, the same help, and the same promises from God.

Point 2 is that the **message is accessible and welcoming to everyone.** There is not a person that you will ever meet who cannot benefit and be moved by the Spirit of the Lord as you share His Word. That message is accessible and we must continue to spread it throughout the world, especially into remote regions where people don't have internet access or buildings to worship in. We do that through people. You and I are living letters. We can get just about anywhere and we can welcome everyone that comes across our path.

We are the light of the world and especially during this season we need to let that light enhance, enlighten, and expose hope, revelation, and truth.

Point 3 is huge. I like this tasty morsel. Paul was not the sharpest tool in the shed when it came to spreading the message and teaching the principles. But the fact was that **God saw that he was equipped.** Though he was the least qualified, and maybe not naturally gifted, he recognized that when Christ lives in you there is a supernatural gifting. It's where the ordinary becomes extraordinary. And point 3 merges with point 4, because once you recognize that God has equipped you, there needs to be action.

Point 4 is when Paul says, "**so here I am. . . .**" I'm talking about things and writing about things that are clearly over my head! It's difficult to wrap your head around the inexhaustible riches of Christ and His generosity. But that *is* the message that is accessible, that *is* the reason we are equipped with abilities and resources. So here we are, ready to be "meat for the Master's use," tools in the hand of the Lord, clay being molded by the Potter. Each of us has a role to play. This is not a secret—it is revealed to those that choose to walk with Christ. We have a task.

Point 5 defines it. **My task is to bring out in the open and make plain.** It's what God has been doing all along. This is why we have missionaries, churches on every corner, spirit-filled music, and spiritually enlightened authors. It's why this word **illuminate** means so much to our church and me. To *be* the light is our task; to bring this life-changing Word out into the open and make it understandable to those within our circle of influence.

Your purpose and ministry could be compared to the wonderful trays of tasty treats that we have had here. You don't do the baking and make dozens of cookies to eat them all yourself. It's a great season to be hospitable, a great time to spread good cheer, and it's always the right time to share the message. Are you willing to share?

Cookie #8

Galatians 1:1-7 AMP

Paul, an apostle—[special messenger appointed and commissioned and sent out] not from [any body of] men nor by or through [a]any man, but by and through Jesus Christ (the Messiah) and God the Father, Who raised Him from among the dead—

And all the brethren who are with me, to the churches of Galatia:

Grace and spiritual blessing be to you and [soul] peace from God the Father and our Lord Jesus Christ (the Messiah),

Who gave (yielded) Himself up [[b]to atone] for our sins [and [c] to save and sanctify us], in order to rescue and deliver us from this present wicked age and world order, in accordance with the will and purpose and plan of our God and Father—

To Him [be ascribed all] the glory through all the ages of the ages and the eternities of the eternities! Amen (so be it).

I am surprised and astonished that you are so quickly [d]turning renegade and deserting Him Who invited and called you [e]by the grace (unmerited favor) of Christ (the Messiah) [and that you are transferring your allegiance] to a different [even an opposition] gospel.

Not that there is [or could be] any other [genuine Gospel], but there are [obviously] some who are troubling and disturbing and bewildering you [[f]with a different kind of teaching which they offer as a gospel] and want to pervert and distort the Gospel of Christ (the Messiah) [into something which it absolutely is not].

*P*aul felt commissioned by God for service. Oh, that we would all feel that same passion! He poured his heart and his life into every message, every city he visited, and every home that he stayed in. He not only had his heart in it, that heart was sold out because of what Christ had done (vs. 4). *It is the purpose and plan of God that we all come to the realization that we are in need of a savior.* To Him be the glory forever and ever!

As my kids get older it is harder and harder to surprise them during the holidays. There used to be a day when they had such anticipation of Christmas morning and had no idea what was coming and then when they saw it, the joy was indescribable. You saw it *and* you heard it in their screams! I must confess that as the years went by, Santa-fever started to diminish. Don't get me wrong, we still have fun, but it's different now. Things change.

Paul experienced something that most people who have ever stayed in church for any length of time face. Renegade believers. Christian deserters. People walking away from faith in God for hope in something or someone else. Paul said that he was surprised and astonished!

In the day we live in and with all of the cultural and social shifts, people seem to gravitate to whatever makes them feel the best. Sometimes the "unmerited favor" of God loses out to "instant gratification" of self. The only way to keep from getting caught up in this is to keep your eyes fixed on something that is constant and consistent. You say, "why do I need to stay focused on Christ?"

Because evil is alive and it seeks vulnerability. It seeks ignorance. It seeks depressed and discouraged folks who have disconnected from life and isolated themselves. It's in these seasons that people become troubled, which leads to them being disturbed and ultimately bewildered. Finally the gospel that they are following is not even the gospel at all. It's distorted, even at times perverted.

You won't always have that fresh baked cookie smell going on in your spiritual kitchen. Sometimes there is a spillover and the oven or the range has a different aroma. I've got this can that I use whenever something surprises me and spills over in my oven. It's called Easy Off. You spray it on; you wipe it off.

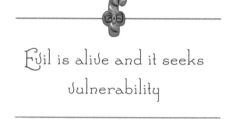

Evil is alive and it seeks vulnerability

And when you do it right, it looks like there was never any mess there at all. I wish there was a can like this for struggles and temptation and trials that come upon us: Easy Off! A little spray and it would go away!

Perhaps that is what the **grace** of God is. That unmerited favor—you just get it, you could not have done enough to earn it. It's unmerited. We need more passionate souls like

Paul; more people who love to cook and see what comes from all the wonderful recipes found in the Word of God. Don't get sidetracked. Stay focused. Watch what you are doing and most importantly, keep your eyes on the prize! His **grace** is sufficient!

Philippians 1:2-11

Grace and peace to you from God our Father and the Lord Jesus Christ.

I thank my God every time I remember you. In all my prayers for all of you, I always pray with joy because of your partnership in the gospel from the first day until now, being confident of this, that he who began a good work in you will carry it on to completion until the day of Christ Jesus.

It is right for me to feel this way about all of you, since I have you in my heart and, whether I am in chains or defending and confirming the gospel, all of you share in God's grace with me. God can testify how I long for all of you with the affection of Christ Jesus.

And this is my prayer: that your love may abound more and more in knowledge and depth of insight, so that you may be able to discern what is best and may be pure and blameless for the day of Christ, filled with the fruit of righteousness that comes through Jesus Christ—to the glory and praise of God.

In 2010 we used as a theme for the year one of the most incredible words the Lord had ever given to our church. The word was "tenacious." To make it even more special, it was our *ten*-year anniversary—our decade of dreams. So many amazing things happened that year for every one of us. As I was thinking about this little edible treat from the Word of God, the little phrase in verse 4 popped out at me, "I always pray with *joy*." To be honest, I do not always pray with joy. I wanted to know why, so I asked the Lord, "why did this pop out at me and why am I not always praying with *Joy*? Who is she anyway? I want to meet her!"

I need to believe that He will finish the things that He starts in me and with me.

As happens most times when I pray, there was no audible voice, no thunder or lighting, so I just continued to read on. And like the sweet warm feeling I get when those hot Tollhouse cookies come right out of the oven, there in verse 6, I bit into the secret that could transform my prayer life. Let's read it again:

Being confident of this, that he who began a good work in you will carry it on to completion until the day of Christ Jesus.

What was the answer to my question regarding why I don't always pray with joy? I realized that my "confidence" level might not have been where it should be. Confidence comes from knowing that what I am praying for or about is in the heart and on the mind of Christ. I began to wonder if I don't sometimes pray things that I already know are not in the will of the Father—they are in the will of *me*. If my prayers have no foundation, if they have not been saturated by a lifestyle that honors God, then I may miss the mark in prayer and in my life.

1 John 5:14-15 says, "This is the confidence we have in approaching God: that if we ask anything according to his will, he hears us. And if we know that he hears us—whatever we ask—we know that we have what we asked of him."

I must know (believe with all my heart) that the Lord hears me when I pray. If I believe that, and if I am asking *anything* according to his will, I should see my confidence grow. But that's just a part of the recipe. *I need to believe that He will finish the things that He starts in me and with me.* I do not want to run out of steam this year. I want to be more and more TENacious. I want to give more to the Lord this month than I have in any month prior. I want to finish strong. Why does it matter?

Let me share a simple, yet easily understood illustration. Sometime ago I went into our sound booth to get out one of the DVDs of a past service to view. As I put it into the player, nothing happened. I could not tell what was wrong so I asked some questions and realized that this DVD had not yet been "finalized." I could look at the back of the disc and see clearly that something was on it but because it had not been "finalized" it was as if nothing had ever been recorded. So I "finalized" it. After it was finished there was a little warning that popped up with another great life lesson: "no recording allowed after finalizing." That's a tasty little treat there, isn't it?

You and I have some things in our lives that may need finalizing. There are some events and circumstances that have not yet been finished and those difficulties seem to always show up in our heads over and over again. There needs to be closure. If it happened to you, it was working in you so that Jesus Christ could show up strong through you in the future. That disc needs to be finalized. You need to close the chapter on that season and let your confidence rise knowing that the Lord will wrap it up, put a bow on it and then give you a brand new day—a fresh start to the best part.

And this is my prayer [with joy]: that your love may abound more and more in knowledge and depth of insight, so that you may be able to discern what is best and may be pure and blameless for the day of Christ, filled with the fruit of righteousness that comes through Jesus Christ—to the glory and praise of God.

I pray with joy because my confidence is in Him. He (Jesus) who began this good work in *you*, will be faithful to carry it on to completion. You can finish strong.

We are TENacious!

Cookie #10

Galatians 4:4-6 NLT

But when the right time came, God sent his Son, born of a woman, subject to the law. God sent him to buy freedom for us who were slaves to the law, so that he could adopt us as his very own children. And because we are his children, God has sent the Spirit of his Son into our hearts, prompting us to call out, "Abba, Father."

What YOU Need to Know This Christmas

Hopefully by now, we are all officially in *Christmas* mode! We are developing a lifestyle of boldness and generosity that is preparing us for what is coming in the New Year. God has a plan for us—a plan for YOU and your family according to His Word.

But I want you to imagine what was happening in this moment. You find this story in Luke chapter 1. Mary's got a boyfriend named Joseph. In the heavenly realm there was a dispatching of Gabriel (messenger angel) to announce to Mary what was "going" to happen. So Gabriel goes to her and tells her something that *you* need to hear this morning:

"You are highly favored and the Lord is with you!"

The first thing I want you to know is that **"the Lord *is* with *you*."** It is very difficult to live in discouragement or fear if you *know* that the Lord is with you. The reason many people suffer or find themselves in despair is because they think they are alone. You are *not* alone! The Lord is with you!

Understandably, Mary was a bit startled by all of this. It's not everyday that an angel drops down in splendor to tell you that you're awesome! But Gabe did. "Mary, you're awesome!"

Mary was greatly troubled at his words and wondered what kind of greeting this might be. But the angel said to her, "Do not be afraid, Mary; you have found favor with God" (Luke 1:29-30).

You are highly favored and the Lord is with you!

You know that your life is about to change when you "find favor." In reality, I'm not sure that you find it—I kind of believe that favor finds you. In *Webster's Dictionary* the definition of favor includes, "friendly or kind regard; good will; approval; liking; unfair partiality; favoritism; attractiveness; to be partial to; prefer; to help; assist; to do a kindness for." To be favored means: "regarded or treated with favor; provided with advantages; specially privileged."

You are walking with God. He is with you and His blessing, His anointing, and His peace are all over you. You are living *courageously* with special privileges! It makes me want to shout!

Can I just say to you that when you realize and accept the fact that Jesus will never leave you or walk out of your life, you will find a place of special provision and special protection. You have found favor! Not just favor with God—you will have favor with people too!

Mary was still confused by this "divine interruption." How do you know that God is there and that His favor is upon you? Read on:

"You will conceive and give birth to a son, and you are to call him Jesus. He will be great and will be called the Son of the Most High. The Lord God will give him the throne of his father David, and he will reign over Jacob's descendants forever; his kingdom will never end" (Luke 1:31-33).

"Mary, God is with you, His favor is all over you and guess what, you are going to have a baby!"

"Say what? I just have a boyfriend . . . I'm not married. How is this possible?"

"How will this be," Mary asked the angel, "since I am a virgin?"

The angel answered, "The Holy Spirit will come on you, and the power of the Most High will overshadow you. So the holy one to be born will be called the Son of God. Even Elizabeth your relative is going to have a child in her old age, and she who was said to be unable to conceive is in her sixth month. For no word from God will ever fail" (Luke 1:34-37).

You need to believe what God says about you. He promised to be with you *in* the midst of everything that you are facing. He promised to bless you with special grace, strength, and resources to do what you will need to do. And you can believe what he says because **no word from God will ever fail!**

There is strength in the name of the Lord; power in the name of the Lord. *Blessed* is he who comes in the name of the Lord. Jesus isn't coming. He's here. You need to invite Him to live in your heart today. Ask Him to save you; to fill you with that spirit that is able to birth something in you that you had nothing to do with. You need to agree with the plan that God has for you. Mary did.

"I am the Lord's servant," Mary answered. *"May your word to me be fulfilled." Then the angel left her* (Luke 1:38).

Mary, ordinary and average Mary, representing all of us who are just living our lives and doing what we know to do—Mary is interrupted by God and everything changes. She was filled with *the* promise, with power and joy and a hope for *all* people. When we live like this we become powerful tools in the hands of God to do great things. Not only will it bring about change in you but you will bring out the best in others too.

At that time Mary got ready and hurried to a town in the hill country of Judea, where she entered Zechariah's home and greeted Elizabeth. When Elizabeth heard Mary's greeting, the baby leaped in her womb, and Elizabeth was filled with the Holy Spirit. In a loud voice she exclaimed: "Blessed are you among women, and blessed is the child you will bear! But why am I so favored, that the mother of my Lord should come to me? As soon as the sound of your greeting reached my ears, the baby in my womb leaped for joy. Blessed is she who has believed that the Lord would fulfill his promises to her!" **(Luke 1:39-45)**

Your words become His *Word* and those things that He longs to birth in others leap whenever you come into the room! You bring out His favor in others!

The right time has come . . . that time is now. You can be divinely interrupted today and your life can dramatically change for the best. Don't be troubled. Don't be afraid. Know this:

The Lord is with **you**.

You have found **favor.**

No Word from the Lord will ever fail. Oh . . . and **you're awesome**!

Colossians 3:1-4 NLT

Since you have been raised to new life with Christ, set your sights on the realities of heaven, where Christ sits in the place of honor at God's right hand. Think about the things of heaven, not the things of earth. For you died to this life, and your real life is hidden with Christ in God. And when Christ, who is your life, is revealed to the whole world, you will share in all his glory.

What Paul is describing here to the church in Colossae is that being saved—being a fully devoted follower of Christ— ought to make you different. Your perspective should be new; your thoughts should be positive and uplifting. When you *know* this you can *grow* in this.

And when Christ, who is your life, is revealed to the whole world, you will share in all his glory (v. 4).

What happened in you needs to be expressed through you so that it can happen because of you for others. Your goal is to share it! When you become "transformed" there is a spiritual metamorphosis that occurs. You come out of your shell. You are a *new* creation. And that changes how you go about living your life. Without Christ coming alive in your life and living in you there will never be real transformation.

So put to death the sinful, earthly things lurking within you. Have nothing to do with sexual immorality, impurity, lust, and evil desires. Don't be greedy, for a greedy person is an idolater, worshiping the things of this world. Because of these sins, the anger of God is coming. You used to do these things when your life was still part of this world. But now is the time to get rid of anger, rage, malicious behavior, slander, and dirty language. Don't lie to each other, for you have stripped off your old sinful nature and all its wicked deeds. Put on your new nature, and be renewed as you learn to know your Creator and become like him. In this new life, it doesn't matter if you are a Jew or a Gentile, circumcised or uncircumcised, barbaric, uncivilized, slave, or free. Christ is all that matters, and he lives in all of us. (Colossians 3:5-11 NLT)

The spiritual life is not about all that you lose or all that you take off. It has everything to do with what you put on. We are always talking about putting on the whole armor so that you will be able to stand against what comes against you. When the cold winds of life begin to blow, you need to "bundle" up. In fact they tell you to put on "layers" of clothing. The layered look not only works physically, it works spiritually!

Since God chose you to be the holy people he loves, you must clothe yourselves *with tenderhearted mercy, kindness, humility, gentleness, and patience.* (Colossians 3:12 NLT)

Now that seems to be a great looking outfit to me. Think about these layers. **Tenderhearted mercy and kindness** . . . sort of like a sweater and scarf combination. There's nothing quite as colorful and captivating as one of those infamous Christmas sweaters and when you combine it with a colorful Christmas scarf . . . well that's how we begin living this wonderful life! Scripture says to bind mercy and truth around your neck. **Humility** can be the cap/hat—you humble yourself. Get your hat on, cover your ears. Your hat, like the helmet of salvation, is what people will notice about you. Humble yourself before God and at just the right time He will lift you up! Put on your gloves of **gentleness**, some boots of **patience** and you will be dressed for anything! Right? What could possibly go wrong? Well you are not quite done yet . . . listen to the rest of Paul's counsel.

When the cold winds of life begin to blow
you need to "bundle" up.

Make allowance for each other's faults [don't be so quick to judge], *and forgive anyone who offends you* [this releases you, not them]. *Remember, the Lord forgave you, so you must forgive others. Above all* [after you have put on all the other layers], *clothe yourselves with love, which binds us all together in perfect harmony.* (Colossians 3:13-14 NLT)

Put on your coat. Don't leave home without your coat. **Love**—it covers everything! It's the perfect outer garment.

And let the peace that comes from Christ rule in your hearts. For as members of one body you are called to live in peace. And always be thankful.

Let the message about Christ, in all its richness, fill your lives. Teach and counsel each other with all the wisdom he gives. Sing psalms and hymns and spiritual songs to God with thankful hearts. And whatever you do or say, do it as a representative of the Lord Jesus, giving thanks through him to God the Father. (Colossians 3:15-17)

Grab your coat and let's go!

Matthew 2:1-11

After Jesus was born in Bethlehem in Judea, during the time of King Herod, Magi from the east came to Jerusalem and asked, "Where is the one who has been born king of the Jews? We saw his star when it rose and have come to worship him."

When King Herod heard this he was disturbed, and all Jerusalem with him. When he had called together all the people's chief priests and teachers of the law, he asked them where the Messiah was to be born. "In Bethlehem in Judea," they replied, "for this is what the prophet has written:

"But you, Bethlehem, in the land of Judah, are by no means least among the rulers of Judah; for out of you will come a ruler who will shepherd my people Israel."

Then Herod called the Magi secretly and found out from them the exact time the star had appeared. He sent them to Bethlehem and said, "Go and search carefully for the child. As soon as you find him, report to me, so that I too may go and worship him."

After they had heard the king, they went on their way, and the star

they had seen when it rose went ahead of them until it stopped over the place where the child was. When they saw the star, they were overjoyed. On coming to the house, they saw the child with his mother Mary, and they bowed down and worshiped him. Then they opened their treasures and presented him with gifts of gold, frankincense and myrrh.

I hope that you have been enjoying these edible treats for your body and soul. Taste and see that the Lord is good . . . and so are all of these cookie recipes in the back of this book! I've had them all!

In 2012 we ventured out beyond the traditional Christmas décor to something a bit more crisp and clean and bright

Timing is Everything.

at The Landing. We had never had stars up on our stage, but that year we brought in two huge stars that were lit up with LED lights. These stars prompted me to take a closer look at the Christmas story again. This time, I noticed the star.

He determines the number of the stars and calls them each by name. (Psalm 147:4)

Some things we can see and learn from the star:

1. Perhaps the most distinguishing thing about the star is its light. **The star illuminates the dark sky.** The wise men *saw* the star in the East. There are nights when the sky

is so dark and clear that the light of the stars brightens up the earth. Looking at them always reminds me just how awesome and complex our Creator is. He knows them by name and he knows the exact number of stars that he created.

2. Verse 7 above says, "Then Herod called the Magi secretly and found out from them the exact time the star had appeared." **The star was an indicator of TIME.** To see this clearly all we have to do is go back to Genesis chapter 1:

God made two great lights—the greater light to govern the day and the lesser light to govern the night. He also made the stars. God set them in the vault of the sky to give light on the earth, to govern the day and the night, and to separate light from darkness. And God saw that it was good. And there was evening, and there was morning—the fourth day. (Genesis 1:16-19)

Timing is everything and the star was able to confirm for Herod the events that were about to take place.

3. The most significant thing about the star was the fact that **it provided direction.** The star led the wise men to Jesus.

After they had heard the king, they went on their way, and the star they had seen when it rose went ahead of them until it stopped over the place where the child was. (v. 9)

The star was the reason that the location of Christ was able to be determined. Prior to this event, God had used clouds and pillars of fire to lead His people in the direction and course of their lives. But the star ushered in how to get them to Jesus.

4. The star lit up the sky, determined the time of day and events, and led them to Jesus. Ultimately **the star brought all of the wise men great joy.**

When they saw the star, they were overjoyed. On coming to the house, they saw the child with his mother Mary, and they bowed down and worshiped him. Then they opened their treasures and presented him with gifts of gold, frankincense and myrrh. (vv. 10-11)

Light . . . time . . . direction . . . joy. All things that were brought to us by a star shining in the east.

I, Jesus, have sent My messenger (angel) to you to witness and to give you assurance of these things for the churches (assemblies). I am the Root (the Source) and the Offspring of David, the radiant and brilliant Morning Star. (Revelation 22:16 AMP)

Wise men and women still seek Him. But we don't need to look to the stars, we can look to the One that made the stars! This year, celebrate the people that are in your life and the Savior that makes everything possible. You can **do** all that He says you can do. You can **be** all that He says you can be. Let your holiday be a holy-day and keep **Christ** in Christmas!

You can do all that He says you can do.
You can be all that He says you can be.

Merry Christmas from all of us at The Landing and may you have a blessed and prosperous New Year!

Christmas Cookie Recipes

I **t's Time to Bake!** We hope that you enjoy these recipes straight from the kitchens of some of our Landing families. Feel free to share these edible treats for your body and soul with those that will gather with you during the holidays. And remember, feed your faith and your doubts will starve to death!

Seven-Layer Magic Cookie Bars

- ☐ 1 stick butter
- ☐ 1 cup graham cracker crumbs
- ☐ 1 can sweetened condensed milk
- ☐ 1 pkg. (6 oz.) semi-sweet chocolate morsels
- ☐ 1 pkg. (6 oz.) butterscotch chips
- ☐ 1½ cups flaked coconut
- ☐ 1 cup chopped nuts

Preheat oven to 350° (325° for glass dish).

In a 13 x 9-inch baking pan, melt butter in oven. Sprinkle graham cracker crumbs over it. Mix together and press into pan. Sprinkle with chocolate chips, then butterscotch chips. Sprinkle coconut over this and then pour condensed milk over all. Sprinkle with chopped nuts. Bake for about 30 minutes. Cool and cut into squares.

Snickerdoodles

- [ ] 1 cup butter
- [ ] 1½ cups sugar
- [ ] 2 eggs
- [ ] 2¾ cups flour
- [ ] 2 tsp. cream of tartar
- [ ] 1 tsp. baking soda
- [ ] ¼ tsp. salt

Preheat oven to 400°.

Mix butter, sugar, and eggs. Add remaining ingredients. Roll into balls the size of walnuts. Roll in a mixture of 2 Tbsp. sugar and 2 tsp. cinnamon. Bake on ungreased cookie sheet for 8-10 minutes.

Grandma's Cookies

- ☐ 1 cup butter
- ☐ ½ cup sifted powdered sugar
- ☐ 1 tsp. vanilla
- ☐ 2¼ cups flour
- ☐ ¼ tsp. salt
- ☐ ¾ cup finely chopped pecans

Preheat oven to 300°.

Mix butter, sugar, and vanilla thoroughly. Stir flour and salt together and blend in. Mix in nuts.

After dough is mixed, make into small balls and place on ungreased cookie sheet. Make an indentation in center. Bake at 300° for about 20 minutes or until set. Let cool then fill the indentation with a mixture of powdered sugar and almond extract, thinned with a little milk to the proper consistency to drop off the end of a spoon. Icing can be colored with food coloring.

Chocolate Crinkles

- [ ] 3 eggs
- [ ] 1½ cups granulated sugar
- [ ] 4 ounces unsweetened chocolate, melted
- [ ] ½ cup vegetable oil
- [ ] 2 tsp. baking powder
- [ ] 2 tsp. vanilla
- [ ] 2 cups all-purpose flour
- [ ] sifted confectioners' sugar

Preheat oven to 375°.

In a large mixing bowl, using an electric mixer, beat eggs, sugar, chocolate, oil, baking powder, and vanilla until blended. Beat in as much of the flour with the mixer as possible, stir in the remaining flour. Cover and chill the cookie dough for 2 hours. Shape dough into 1-inch balls. Roll in sifted confectioners' sugar, coating well. Place balls of cookie dough about 1 inch apart on ungreased cookie sheets and bake for 8 to 10 minutes, until crackled in appearance. Transfer cookies to a wire rack to cool. Sprinkle with more confectioners' sugar if desired.

Chocolate Chip Cookies

- ☐ 2¼ cups all-purpose flour
- ☐ 1 tsp. baking soda
- ☐ 1 tsp. salt
- ☐ 1 stick of Crisco baking sticks
- ☐ ¾ cup granulated sugar
- ☐ ¾ cup packed brown sugar
- ☐ 1 tsp. vanilla extract
- ☐ 2 large eggs
- ☐ ½ bag of semi-sweet morsels
- ☐ ½ bag of white chocolate morsels

Preheat oven to 375°.

Combine flour, baking soda, and salt in small bowl. Beat butter, granulated sugar, brown sugar, and vanilla extract in large mixer bowl until creamy. Add eggs, one at a time, beating well after each addition. Gradually beat in flour mixture. Stir in morsels. Drop by rounded tablespoon onto ungreased baking sheets. Bake 9 to 11 minutes. Cool on baking sheet.

Peanut Blossom Cookies

- ☐ 1 8 oz. bag Hershey's kisses, unwrapped
- ☐ ½ cup shortening (oleo or butter)
- ☐ ¾ cup peanut butter
- ☐ ½ cup granulated sugar
- ☐ ½ cup packed light brown sugar
- ☐ 1 egg
- ☐ 2 Tbsp. milk
- ☐ 1 tsp. vanilla
- ☐ 1½ cups all-purpose flour
- ☐ 1 tsp. baking soda
- ☐ ½ tsp. salt
- ☐ Granulated sugar

Preheat oven to 375°.

Beat shortening and peanut butter in large bowl until well blended. Add ½ cup granulated sugar and brown sugar; beat until fluffy. Add egg, milk, and vanilla; beat well. Stir together flour, baking soda, and salt; gradually beat into peanut butter mixture. Shape dough into 1-inch balls. Roll in granulated sugar; place on ungreased cookie sheet. Bake 8 to 10 minutes or until lightly browned. Immediately press a kiss into center of each cookie; cookie will crack around edges. Cool completely.

Oreo Balls

- ☐ 1 package regular size Oreo cookies, crushed
- ☐ 1 (8 oz.) package cream cheese, softened
- ☐ 1 pkg. white almond bark
- ☐ 1 pkg. chocolate almond bark

Using a blender or handheld mixer, mix Oreos and cream cheese. Roll into walnut size balls. Chill for an hour.

Melt approximately ¾ package of white almond bark. Stick a toothpick in ball and dip it in the melted almond bark. Allow to harden on wax paper, takes about 15 min.

While waiting, melt about ¼ package of chocolate almond bark.

When Oreo balls are no longer sticky to the touch, decorate with drizzles of chocolate and white almond bark. Use a sandwich bag with a tiny hole, cut one corner to drizzle the almond bark.

No-Bake Nutella Peanut Butter Cookies

- ☐ 3 Tbsp. butter
- ☐ ½ cup granulated sugar
- ☐ ¼ cup milk
- ☐ 1 Tbsp. unsweetened cocoa powder
- ☐ ¼ cup peanut or hazelnut butter
- ☐ ¾ cup Nutella hazelnut spread
  (or 1 cup chocolate chips)
- ☐ 2 Tbsp. hazelnut liqueur
  (such as Frangelico – optional)
- ☐ 2 cups rolled oats

In a medium to large saucepan, melt the butter over medium to medium-low heat. Add the sugar, milk, and cocoa powder and mix until combined. Stir in the peanut butter, Nutella, and Frangelico until melted, followed by the oats. Continue mixing until all of the ingredients are incorporated.

Reduce heat to lowest setting.

Working quickly, scoop to shape of balls and place them on a parchment-lined sheet pan. Refrigerate for thirty minutes until firm. Store in an airtight container. Makes 2 dozen.

Pretzel Turtles

- ☐ 20 small mini pretzels
- ☐ 20 chocolate covered caramel candies
  (Rolo's are recommended)
- ☐ 20 pecan halves

Preheat oven to 300°.

Arrange the pretzels in a single layer on a parchment lined cookie sheet. Place one chocolate covered caramel candy on top of each pretzel.

Bake for 4 minutes. While the candy is still warm, press a pecan half onto each candy covered pretzel. Cool completely before storing in an airtight container.

Chocolate Malted Cookies

- ☐ 2 cups packed brown sugar
- ☐ ¾ cup malted milk powder (such as Carnation)
- ☐ 10 Tbsp. butter, softened
- ☐ 6 Tbsp. chocolate syrup
- ☐ 2 Tbsp. vanilla extract
- ☐ 2 large eggs
- ☐ 4 cups all-purpose flour
- ☐ 2 tsp. baking soda
- ☐ 1 tsp. salt
- ☐ 1 cup milk chocolate chips
- ☐ 2/3 cup semisweet chocolate mini-chips

Preheat oven to 350°.

Combine first 6 ingredients in a large bowl; beat with a mixer at medium speed for 2 minutes or until light and fluffy. Lightly spoon flour into dry measuring cups; level with a knife. Combine flour, baking soda, and salt in a medium bowl; stir with a whisk. Gradually add flour mixture to sugar mixture, beating at low speed until well blended. Stir in the milk chocolate chips and semisweet chocolate mini-chips. Drop dough by heaping teaspoonfuls 2 inches apart onto baking sheets. Bake for 10 minutes. Cool on pans 2 minutes or until firm. Remove cookies from pans; cool on wire racks. Yield: 5 dozen cookies.

Ginger Snaps

- ☐ ¾ cup shortening
- ☐ ¾ cup packed brown sugar
- ☐ 1 egg
- ☐ ¾ cup molasses
- ☐ 3 cups flour
- ☐ 2 tsp. baking soda
- ☐ 1 tsp. cinnamon
- ☐ ¼ tsp. salt
- ☐ ½ tsp. cloves
- ☐ 1 tsp. ginger

Preheat oven to 375°.

Cream together shortening and brown sugar. Add egg and molasses; mix well and set aside. Sift all other ingredients until well blended and add flour mixture to first mixture. Chill mixture to allow for easier shaping. Once chilled, shape into small balls. Roll in powdered sugar and bake for 12 minutes.

Pumpkin Cookies

COOKIES:

- ☐ 1½ cups sugar
- ☐ ½ cup oil
- ☐ 1 can pumpkin
- ☐ 1½ tsp. cinnamon
- ☐ 1 tsp. cloves
- ☐ 1½ tsp. vanilla
- ☐ 3 cups flour
- ☐ 1½ tsp. baking soda
- ☐ 1½ tsp. baking powder
- ☐ ½ cup nuts
- ☐ 1 cup raisins

Preheat oven to 375°.

Mix sugar, oil, vanilla, and pumpkin. Slowly add spices, flour, soda, and baking powder. Mix thoroughly. Fold in raisins and nuts. Drop on greased cookie sheet. Bake for 10-15 minutes. Do not over-bake.

(ICING INSTRUCTIONS NEXT PAGE)

Pumpkin Cookies (cont'd)

ICING:

- ☐ 6 Tbsp. butter
- ☐ 8 tsp. milk
- ☐ 1 cup brown sugar
- ☐ 1 tsp. vanilla
- ☐ 2 – 2½ cups powdered sugar

Cook butter, milk, brown sugar, and vanilla over low heat until mixture is smooth. Remove from heat and add powdered sugar. Beat until smooth. Frost cookies as soon as they can be handled.

About the Author

Joe began managing non-profits as Executive Director of Carman Ministries, Inc. in the early 80's. In 2000, after more than 1000 live events and multiple achievements with Carman, he began an organization called Dreams2Destiny Center, which helped people identify their talents/calling and move towards what they were designed to do. In 2002, Joe founded The Landing Community Church where he was Lead Pastor until June of 2015. Presently he serves at Gateway Church in Southlake, Texas. Author of eight books and father of three grown children, Joe continues helping churches and organizations clarify their focus, enlarge their vision and pursue their dreams.

Website: cupofjoe.tv

Instagram: cupofjoetv

Twitter: cupofjoetv

Facebook: cupofjoetv

Audio and Video Files: media.cupofjoe.tv

ALSO AVAILABLE

CH8NGE?

Know... Grow... Go When It's Time

JOE JONES